Proof of Identity

NEIL POWELL was born in London in 1948 and educated at Sevenoaks School and the University of Warwick. He has taught English, owned a bookshop and, since 1990, been a full-time author and editor. His books include six previous collections of poetry – *At the Edge* (1977), *A Season of Calm Weather* (1982), *True Colours* (1990), *The Stones on Thorpeness Beach* (1994), *Selected Poems* (1998) and *A Halfway House* (2004) – as well as *Carpenters of Light* (1979), *Roy Fuller: Writer and Society* (1995), *The Language of Jazz* (1997), all published by Carcanet Press, and *George Crabbe: An English Life* (Pimlico, 2004) and *Amis & Son: Two Literary Generations* (Macmillan, 2008). His centenary life of Benjamin Britten will appear in 2013. He lives in Suffolk.

Also by Neil Powell from Carcanet Press

NEIL POWELL

Proof of Identity

CARCANET

First published in Great Britain in 2012 by
Carcanet Press Limited
Alliance House
Cross Street
Manchester M2 7AQ

www.carcanet.co.uk

A CIP catalogue record for this book is available from the British Library

ISBN 978 1 84777 095 0

The publisher acknowledges financial assistance from Arts Council England

Typeset in Monotype Garamond by XL Publishing Services, Tiverton
Printed and bound in England by SRP Ltd, Exeter

For Stuart and Jane Affleck

Acknowledgements

Some of these poems have previously appeared in *PN Review*, *Poetry Review*, *The Rialto* and *The Spectator*. The opening lines of 'Knole' refer to Robert Sackville-West's *Inheritance: The Story of Knole and the Sackvilles* (Bloomsbury, 2010). 'Louis Takes a Break' is about Louis Armstrong's first recorded solo, in 'Chimes Blues' by King Oliver's Creole Jazz Band (7 April 1923). 'The Journal of Lily Lloyd' preserves as closely as possible the vocabulary of my grandmother's original notebook, adapted and rearranged into eleven-syllable lines; my thanks are due to Chris Eldridge for correcting several errors in an earlier draft. 'A Huntingdonshire Elegy' gratefully borrows its form and title from John Greening's 'Huntingdonshire Elegies' (*Hunts: Poems 1979–2009*, Greenwich Exchange, 2009), with the author's permission.

Contents

Proof of Identity

What he kept showed what he was: passports,
Wartime identity card, rare photographs
Snapped on his business travels or, much later on,
As a tired and portly district councillor.

He'd be leaving for work: polishing his shoes,
Checking his silk tie, kissing his wife goodbye;
A dewy garden carnation in his buttonhole,
His handkerchief folded to its alpine peak.

Or returning: *News* and *Standard* flung aside,
Reaching for the decanter, the evening's first sherry,
Smelling of the world and his smoky journey home –
The last steam train from London Bridge to Reigate.

Then he'd be away for days or weeks at a time,
Piecing together Europe's shattered glassware,
His passports crammed with kaleidoscopic visas;
The People's Republic of Yugoslavia takes a page.

It's Belgium and Holland mostly: his closest friends
The Wautys and the Dehandschutters of Manage,
And always, in Maastricht, the Mager Brothers
Who sounded, I thought, like something out of films.

And surely Willy Mager took these photographs,
In their continental treacle-tinted colour:
My father relaxed, ironic, in command,
Looking for once the statesman he should have been.

My mother's with him (I'm packed off at school),
More beautiful and happier than I remember her
On the emotional see-saw of our life at home.
It strikes me now that she's in love: with whom?

Unanswerable still. She stayed loyal to her man,
The father I've come too late to understand,
As I rummage through these remnants of identity:
His passports, a few photographs, and me.

The Lindshammar Pig

This glassblower's cheeks are bulbous as Dizzy Gillespie's
As he forms what must surely be a blue glass flask.
He'll add four feet, two ears, blob eyes, a curly tail,
And seal the aperture to create a stumpy snout.

But in truth he's ruined it: that slit along the back
Turns it into a piggy-bank, a glowing deep-blue toy.
'It would be great as a pig, without the slit,' says the boy.
'Okay' – and the glassblower smiles – 'for you I make one.'

We have come to Vetlanda, in the east of Sweden,
By slow train from cabbage-coloured Gothenburg,
Steaming in a warm wet summer. Some long hours later,
The pig is boxed and cotton-woolled, safe for its journey.

Caught in a North Sea storm, the ferry runs six hours late;
His mother brings the seasick boy a peach, then eats it.
Asked at Tilbury Customs, 'Anything to declare?'
The boy replies winningly: 'Yes, I have a blue pig.'

Now the Lindshammar pig surveys a Suffolk snowfield
And everybody from that day in Vetlanda is dead,
Except for the boy and, in a manner of speaking, the pig.
If there's an afterlife, the glassblower will be smiling.

Hotel Codan

With its perkily assertive fifties lowercase 'd',
The hotel's sign has just gone out of date.
Otherwise, it's as the man from Tuborg said:
All glassy restraint, and the best view in town.

I must earn the freedom of this Nordic city,
Its green oxidised roofs and gulping gargoyles.
The English bookshop has next month's Penguins,
But I'm learning new words: *smørrebrød, pilsner, duvet*.

On a pleasure boat cruising the blue canals,
An olive-skinned boy my age is collecting fares:
Youthful outsiders, we exchange complicit smiles.
Lights dance in the water by the floating tattooist.

Dinner tonight in the rooftop restaurant
Where an elderly pianist, Viennese and dapper,
Plays lollipops spiked with melancholia.
Old Europe's sadness drifts on the darkened sea.

Me and Mr Jones

One side of Church Street was a bombed crater,
Fenced off with wonky posts and wire netting,
Torn and distorted like an old string vest:
We'd chuck pebbles from the school crocodile.

Across the street, where the Old Wheel teashop
Tottered genteelly, an anonymous parade:
Outfitter, off-licence, grocer, estate agent,
And RHYTHM, that strange unspellable word.

I'd park my bike against the double-stepped kerb
Outside the record shop. The manager, Mr Jones,
Crinkly-haired and smelling of the wardrobe,
Greeted me like an old friend. I was ten years old.

Did he guess at his corrupting influence?
I think he simply saw a fellow addict
To pamper with free catalogues and supplements,
Spare cardboard sleeves or bargain-price deletions.

Most of what I'd buy was junkshop stuff,
Threepence or sixpence, but sometimes I'd save up
Until I had the astonishing six bob
To become a paying customer of Mr Jones.

The little pegboard-walled audition room:
Last year's top twenties dangling from a pin,
Frayed posters for forgotten pantomimes,
Giant portraits – Mantovani, Vera Lynn –

Caught on the cusp of the almost obsolete;
The steady electric hum, emphatic click
Of sapphire to shellac as the pick-up dropped
On the latest by Elvis or the Everlys.

Then the purchase made, the record wrapped
In its red-and-white-striped bag proclaiming
There is no form of music without Rhythm,
Lovingly nursed through its two-wheeled journey,

Hugged to my shed at the bottom of the garden,
Played there to a captive audience of ants
(A bright new needle in my wind-up HMV),
Catalogued and shelved. I see a habit,

Lifelong, clearly forming. More than that:
The fragile thing, brought safely home to cherish,
Had a sort of sacred magic which would vanish
When discs were vinyl, gramophones plugged in.

The Break

Woodsmoke and dusk can always bring it on,
That September evening fifty years ago:
Absurd in my crisp new suit from Horncastle's,
A starched white collar and a silly striped tie,
Pretending I was something I wasn't quite yet.

The road through Godstone, Oxted, Westerham;
At Riverhead, the church perched on its hill;
A long town, yew trees and a gravelled drive;
Unloading cars and big uncurtained windows;
Inside, a crush of notice-boards and scurrying.

Then, snatched goodbyes in the hessian-covered hall.
I should have said: 'I'm not staying here.
These people are mad. We're going home.'
My mother would have said: 'You know he's right.'
And my father: 'If you're sure that's what you want…'

The grey Wolseley would have swept over the gravel,
Through the gates, down Tubs Hill, into open country;
Lit villages would have glowed with benediction,
And soon we'd have been home, laughing and weeping
Over a scratch supper of bacon and eggs.

Instead, towards the middle of second prep
Each evening, I'd imagine them sitting down
To dinner, and my empty place at the table,
With a vase, perhaps, or a wine bottle or the cruet
To fill the space where my own plate should have been.

One wrong turning can mess up all your life.
It's taken me fifty years to see that this was it,
The break that left me forever disconnected.
I hoped that it would all come right at Christmas,
With presents or prayer, but of course it never did.

At the Piano

June 1/64.   To: S/H Grand Piano in Rosewood Case by Cramer.   £140–0–0.

I

Facing familiar letters, inlaid, uppercase –
CRAMER LONDON – I glimpse their burnished gold
Gleaming in a showroom. The year is 1912.

Grand double doors admit potential buyers.
Will they affront the air with dissonance from Vienna?
Or risk some ragtime? No, tryers-out play safe,

Meandering through a simple drawing-room ballad,
Wrestling with Chopin, ending with Chopsticks.
A show-off might tinker with Rachmaninov.

The men carry hats, the ladies parasols. Outside,
New Bond Street is sunlit, great wars unimagined.
And the piano, unflappable as a salesman, sings.

2

A period of use, long years of beauty-sleep,
Then restoration in a Kentish village.
It's the last straw for the piano-tuner's wife:
'George, if you don't get rid of it, I'm leaving.'

Their little house is rattling with pianos –
This one, his favourite, clogging up the garage.
Almost in tears, he sells it to my father,
Who says it will be used (his son is learning).

3

It's taken half a lifetime and a death
To reunite us both: my piano and I.

And the music: *Master Series for the Young,*
The Eclipse Series of Artistic Albums…

My piano-teacher's tactful fingerings
No longer fit these same but different hands.

His pencilled dates assert my competence
At this baffling Beethoven in 1963.

Well, I must practise, try at last to grasp
What once I understood imperfectly.

4

One friend disputes the sovereignty of keys.
I counter with the obvious example:
A sonata's plangent song of C sharp minor
Transposed a semitone down to C just dies.

But what about the moonlight rivalry,
Debussy's all flats and Beethoven's all sharps,
Same notes to play yet given different names
And therefore sounding different: how can this be?

No less incongruous, the shock of sameness:
That dour A flat supporting middle C
Which starts the *Pathétique*'s adagio
Is the first chord of Ellington's 'Mood Indigo'.

5

Sometimes at night I hear a ghost-piano
Played by Winifred Atwell or Russ Conway,
Its out-of-tuneness a reproachful echo;

Or else recall my teacher's old black Bechstein,
The ivories scabbed and ridged like fingernails,
The treble sweet as Rubinstein's or Curzon's.

At other times, the dream-perspective alters
And views the instrument on a different scale:
Beneath the lid, a gym for tiny creatures

Who vault over the dampers, safely landing
On soft blue felt before they scale the pegs.
How did anyone envisage such a thing?

6

Piano Malcolm frowns: ill-tempered clavier.
Its sins no worse than age and wilfulness,
It hates the central heating and the weather.

Now Malcolm tells me that my piano's thirsty:
He prescribes a bowl of water underneath.
The cat looks puzzled, then laps gratefully.

Kempas Highway, 1966

Steady rain, and the wipers' shuffling beat
Smudges streetlamps and the passing cars
Into a slurry of extruded light.
The city centre with its crowds and bars –
Down to the next junction, then turn right –
Seems as remote and washed-out as the stars.

And so at Kenilworth Road, the signals red,
I hug the nearside lane, the way I'll go
Back to my silent digs and narrow bed;
While Jimmy Ruffin on the radio
Wonders what becomes of the broken-hearted.
I think I could tell him that. I think I know.

For first love never disappears: it sets,
A pearl one neither loses nor forgets.

In Sudbourne Wood

New season's sun: slant light of Aquarius;
Sky-blue shining puddles after days of rain;
Last year's bracken like shattered basketwork;
A sliced-off line of pallid-shanked Scots pines.

On the verge, a fallen bough with a dog's head
Stares up at me from among the alexanders.
A blackbird clacks and flaps at whatever has fired
His tiny anger. I remember the terrible summer.

These are calm days: the damage done repaired,
The account closed, a time to take stock slowly.
In the mid-afternoon distance, mist has gathered
Where the little church is snuggled in its valley.

Parkland

As far as the eye can see:
stately white-painted railings;
cropped grass darkened here and there
by tactful underground streams;
chestnuts, birches, oaks fenced off
or, nearer home, encircled
by slatted wooden benches;
and, in the shadowed distance,
conversational horses.

It stretches back to childhood:
a scattered Surrey village,
cattle-grids and gravelled tracks
the contours of my map;
a wilderness half-contained,
organic and orderly,
trying out its boundaries,
asserting its clarity.
I have always loved parkland.

Knole

The Sackvilles were mostly mad.
This book blames a 'rogue gene' for
that 'slow reclusive despair'
which drove them out of their minds.

Knole was, according to Burke,
'a pleasant habitation…
a grand repository':
oppressive clutter, more like.

But I remember the park
from winter afternoon runs:
setting off close to the gates,
rapidly losing the pack,

veering away to the right.
Distant scatter of antlers;
leafmould, twigs snapping, creatures
scuttling; not a soul in sight.

Along the wall of the house,
downhill back to the valley:
the runner's stumbling rhythm
leading to poems like this.

Blackborough Park

At the bus stop by the iron gates, a man steps off
The green double-decker, which trundles away.
He turns towards the park. Ahead, low in the sky,
A sun red as a chilblain glares down on him
And the grubby gravel path bisecting the grass
With its molehills, wormcasts and black muddy edge.

He's a man you've seen before: the kind of man
Who steps off double-deckers, whether green or not,
Wearing a fawn-coloured mac or a dark overcoat,
Balding on top though needing a haircut next week
To sort out that whiskery stuff round his neck and ears,
With scuffed shoes, a scruffy look, up to no good.

Soon the path branches, as he remembers it should.
The right-hand fork climbs towards formal gardens,
South-facing against the north wall and, further along,
Some overgrown allotments. Now he remembers
Brash massed dahlias, yearning michaelmas daisies.
His father brought him here on Saturday mornings.

The left fork dips down into a long shaded avenue:
Wellingtonias or (he searches for the proper word) sequoias,
Century-old striplings, yet already rubbing shoulders.
He chooses this path, despite the autumnal chill;
He likes the way in which sunlight turns to starlight,
Glinting through the leaves and dancing on the ground.

Down there, he thinks, where the avenue ends there's a lake:
He'd feed the ducks, and one summer a pair of swans
Appeared, paraded round, and were never seen again.
But it was late September when, walking home from school,
They dared Richard Bell to swim across and he drowned.
And from that day on the park was out of bounds.

At the opposite gate, almost half a mile away,
There's a girl in a striped woolly scarf, pushing a pram:
A proper old-fashioned pram, with a recurrent squeak
From its nearside rear wheel like a plaintive cat,
And within it a baby in an Edwardian bonnet,
Dozing with an air of perplexed tranquility.

This is strange and not strange: it matches the park,
Which itself seems forged from the indeterminate past.
And the girl herself, despite those horizontal stripes
On the scarf wrapped round and round her long dark hair,
Is a patchwork sort of person; fragments of pattern,
Paisley or Morris, peep from beneath her coat.

If you imagine her house, it has multicoloured rugs,
Hand-embroidered cushions, home-made curtains;
She reads with unfashionable taste – Elizabeth Bowen,
Ivy Compton-Burnett – and cooks well with organics,
Wholefoods; she's a cheerfully lapsing vegetarian.
It is less easy to imagine her husband or partner.

She walks to where paths meet at a tall thin lamppost.
'Pole,' says the child, suddenly waking and staring:
A random first word, perhaps, or an accurate observation.
'Pole,' she repeats dreamily, mostly to herself. 'That's right.'
They are going downhill now, away from the gazebo,
Towards the circle with an obelisk, close to the lake.

She pauses to absorb the sunlit scene before her,
Pointing things out to the child, who nevertheless
Remains obstinately entranced by the gesturing finger.
One day she'll explain how the words round the obelisk
Record the gift of Sir Alfred Blackborough, this park,
In memory of his only son, killed at Mafeking.

On the park's north boundary there's an undulating wall,
A crinkle-crankle wall they'd call it in East Anglia,
And, midway along, a narrow latched wooden door,
Through which Alice might enter her garden of talking flowers;
Although, on the other side, there's an urban back lane,
Rusty bikes and wheelie bins, washing-lines in yards.

The boy in the leather jacket sneaks in with the air
Of someone seeking a quiet windless spot for a fag,
Away from his nagging parents and scrounging sister.
The jacket is ripped – tufts of red lining show through –
And his jeans are stained with blotches of motor oil,
Which is curious for someone who can't afford a car.

He sets off along the little path where in spring
There's an alpine garden and a shady drift of bluebells;
Now there are remnants of colchicum, autumn crocus,
But he doesn't notice them. This segment of the park
Has relics of allotments: a clump of artichokes,
A gnarled tree stooping with its load of small apples.

He doesn't notice because noticing is not what he does:
Clear and purposeful, he would, if he thought about it,
Regard looking and imagining as beside the point.
He's just split with his girlfriend, who's still only fifteen,
And therefore illegal, so it's probably just as well.
He cuts across the cropped grass towards the gazebo.

The gazebo is closed and boarded-up for the winter:
There are torn posters advertising discos, gigs, a circus;
Some bloke from the BNP has put one there as well.
The boy in the leather jacket doesn't stop to read them:
Without so much as a glance, he nips round the back
And in the urine-scented shade he lights his cigarette.

An old lady sits on the knobbly, uncomfortable bench
By the lakeside. The sun, livid and low to her right,
Casts long spiky shadows from nearby leafless trees.
Wrapped up against the cold in a cream woollen coat
And on her head a two-storey cake-shaped hat,
She looks like a chess-piece, the White Queen perhaps.

A quartet of mallards sidles up, with expectant quacks.
She smiles at them helplessly. 'I've nothing for you,'
She tells them, making a forlorn empty-hands gesture.
The ducks paddle off, quite seeming to understand,
Only to dither, circle and return: short-term memory
Possibly not their strong point nor, she concedes, hers.

Indignant at this, she shouts at them fiercely: 'Shoo!'
And they indeed sort of disperse, as she turns
Away from the lake, to glance back along the path
Where a girl pushes a pram as, many years ago,
She did, when the park was young. She smiles once more
At the overlapping image, this strange turning of time.

She thinks: it's an old-fashioned pram, a proper pram,
And it wants a drop of oil. A boy in a leather jacket
Grinds a cigarette butt into the path near the gazebo,
While a man in mac or overcoat suddenly emerges
Into sunlight from the shadowed avenue. She thinks:
They'll all meet at the obelisk. I wonder what will happen.

What happened? Well, of course, I wasn't there,
And can't be expected to know. This is infuriating
But, unlike most things in this story, true. As for the man
From the double-decker bus, the girl with the pram,
The boy in the leather jacket, the old lady on the bench,
The ducks she didn't feed. They were there. They were.

The Boy on the Bus

I am the boy on the bus. Soft milky light
Is gently bathing frantic city streets;
Somewhere a cheerful urban bird is singing.
It's good up here. Things may turn out all right.

I am the boy on the bus. And yet elsewhere,
My friends are now unsafely underground –
As I should be, aboard the Northern Line.
There is no choice: I have to join them there.

I am the boy on the bus. I don't know how
The twists of destiny have brought me here.
I am the boy on the bus. We've turned a corner.
I only know I have to do this now.

July 2005

Strand, 1923

No shadows here: the distance recedes in mist;
A London Particular's inching up the river.
Crowds fill the pavement and the open-topped buses;
One or two of them have read *The Waste Land*.

A poster: 'Break any engagement to see *Ambush*.'
Another suggests a trip to *Little Old New York*.
Handbag beneath her arm, clothes unshowy but good,
Mrs Dalloway passes the Strand Palace Hotel.

And no one has noticed the photographer –
Except, from the back of a horse-drawn covered wagon,
Propped among sacks and packages, the grocer's boy
Smiles shyly at the camera and the future.

Louis Takes a Break

Meanwhile, elsewhere: in Richmond, Indiana,
Seven musicians huddle round a horn
Which, like the Strand's unnoticed camera,
Records the moment. Yes, a star is born.

Because the second cornet's so majestic,
They've put him at the back where he won't drown
Honoré's trombone or Johnny's blackstick;
A wise move, that, until those chimes ring down.

Then something happens: Louis takes a break.
The hot news from America fills our ears:
A sound too proud and noble to mistake,
Through all the wow and flutter of the years.

The Journal of Lily Lloyd

In memory of Dulcie Powell, née Lloyd (1922–2008)

I

The last day of October 1919:
Waterloo Station: not feeling excited,
sort of feeling all upside-down. Quite a crowd
to see us off. In the train to Southampton,
a dear little Scotch boy who'd been to visit
his granny in Scotland and was very pleased
to be going back to the sunshine, saying
such funny native words. We reached Southampton
about 12.30: there was the lovely boat,
the *Balmoral Castle*. What a huge vessel!
There were thirty young married couples on board,
all English girls trying their luck in S.A.
I learnt that I was in a two-berth cabin
with a nice young woman called Mrs Ritchie.
Lunch was laid in the big dining saloon,
the stewards all looking very clean and fresh
in their little white jackets: a lovely lunch,
plenty of everything, huge dishes of fruit.
We were leaning over the side of the boat,
as they were drawing up the landing-bridges,
when a man came alongside taking photos:
he said if I'd throw down a penny ha'penny
he'd send one to my home address in London.

Inserted here, a sepia photograph:
'R.M.S. Balmoral Castle'. There they are:
Lily, in her crumpled fur-trimmed coat and hat
decorated as if with fancy icing,
beams with ingenuous goodness; meanwhile Jack,
in military cap and greatcoat, smiles wryly,
with deep-set eyes, broad nose and semaphore ears.
He looks like me. We meet, after ninety years.

The ropes were being hauled in and the engines
bumping, a dockside band struck up 'Good Byee',
and at last we were moving, oh so slowly;
then the band had changed its tune to 'Auld Lang Syne',
and as you looked along the line of young girls,
all had tears in their eyes. We couldn't help it:
not one of us knew what was in store for us.
Soon we were going full steam ahead, along
the English Channel, and it was almost dark.

What a head I had when I woke next morning!
I felt I couldn't lift it off the pillow.
The stewardess brought cups of tea: awful stuff,
stewed, coloured with what tasted like Ideal Milk,
and with so much sugar we couldn't drink it.
It made Mrs Ritchie sick. Just after that,
her husband came, helped her dress and get on deck.
After a struggle, I dressed and crawled on deck,
staggered to the rail and was terribly ill.
I looked round for Jack but he wasn't up yet:
he wasn't attentive like Mr Ritchie.
The pair of us stayed in this horrible state
until we reached the island of Madeira.

We first saw it looking like a huge black cloud
standing on the water; as we drew nearer,
we could see the hollows in the hills, and trees,
and red, green, blue and white roof tops of houses.
As soon as we anchored in Funchal Harbour,
hundreds of tugs and rowing-boats came to us;
natives clambered up the side of the vessel
like a lot of monkeys, with their wares to sell,
chairs, tables, baskets, hand embroidery work.
There were lots of naked little boys swimming,
shouting to the passengers 'Penny I dive',
diving like fish to get the coins thrown to them.

We were off again: all was merry and bright,
and everyone was well over seasickness.
There were all sorts of games and competitions,

impromptu dances and a fancy dress ball,
a big boxing tournament, and the Three Scamps,
the music hall artistes, gave us several turns.
Monday 16th of November, at 5 a.m.,
we arrived in Cape Town and were woken by
everybody's husband shouting, 'Come and look
at God's own country!' We dressed and went on deck.
A glorious sight it was: Table Mountain
and Lion's Head towering over the docks,
lovely blue sky and not a cloud to be seen.

2

Myself and two other girls were left on board
while our husbands were taken to Maitland Camp
to get their discharge. But then, when Jack came back,
I understood the lies he'd been telling me:
he had deceived us all. He said I must go
at once to the Governor General Fund,
ask for two nights' shelter in Cape Town, rail fares
to Johannesburg and a week's shelter there.
I swear I would never have got off that boat
if it had been leaving again straight away.
But I put my pride in my pocket and went:
I had made my bed and I must lie on it,
and hope for better luck in the Transvaal.

The man at the Governor General Fund
took my hand: 'Do you mean to say you've married
an apprentice fitter and come all this way?
I admire your pluck.' We got our two days' board
at Small's Hotel: a bedroom overlooking
Devil's Peak. That evening, after dinner,
we went round Table Mountain in a tramcar,
arum lilies growing wild along the side;
we also bought some silver leaves from a man,
as we didn't go high enough to pick them.
(Here, four glued-in dried leaves 'off Table Mountain'.)
Next day, we went to Muizenberg – it was there

that I first saw people riding on surfboards –
then to a pretty suburb, Clifton-on-Sea:
Jack was one of those 'live for today' people,
so we decided to make the most of it.

Next morning at ten o'clock we caught the train
to Johannesburg. Those trains are great big things:
each carriage holds six passengers; there are bunks
to let down for sleeping, washbasin, mirror,
card table, even a little balcony
with tip-up seats if you want a breath of air.
It was all lovely and green until we reached
the Great Karoo Plain, a terrible dry stretch,
almost a desert: it took hours to pass through.
There were ostriches and butcher-birds and then
we were crawling round a narrow mountain ledge.
At last, after two days and nights on the train,
we arrived at Park Station, Johannesburg.

We were taken to Long's Hotel where we washed
and had a good breakfast; then Jack decided
to find some of his people. He didn't know
where anyone lived: they are all rolling stones.
But he knew that his niece, a girl of eighteen,
worked at a large draper's shop called Walter Wise,
so we went and found her. Her name was Edie.
She asked for the morning off, took us to meet
her mother, Jack's sister Ivy, then left to fetch
Jack's mother, who didn't seem pleased to see us;
next day, I also met Jack's sister Lily.
I summed them up as rather a funny crowd,
all living in furnished rooms: not one of them
had so much as a stick they could call their own.

I spent a couple of lonely days while Jack
went to one of the gold mines of the East Rand:
he was to start work the following Monday.
We set off for the nearest town, Benoni,
and found a place to live: an unfurnished room
with our own door and a piece of verandah.

Everything was so terribly expensive:
our furniture on the hire purchase system,
a Blue Flame Perfection stove to cook by,
a bicycle for Jack to ride to work on.
If it hadn't been for Jack's kind brother Frank,
who was on the railway in Natal and sent
£5 a month, we should never have pulled through:
from the start, I'd much to thank his brothers for.

One Sunday, after five months in Benoni,
we found that Jack's brother Bert was living there,
running a native eating house. We asked him
to supper: I made my table look lovely
for my first visitor. He was dark and tall,
quite different from Jack; he often popped in,
and persuaded us to take a house with him
in Bedford Street, with three rooms, kitchen, pantry,
bathroom, quite a nice back yard. Then Bert gave us
a present – half a dozen white Leghorn hens
and one rooster – so we'd plenty of fresh eggs.
For the first two months, we got on very well,
until Jack and Bert fell out: Bert decided
he was paying too much, which he was really –
we thought he was trying to help us along –
and so he packed his trunk and went, leaving us
in an awful stew. We had to find the rent,
light and water bills with no one to help out.
We put up a card: 'Unfurnished room to let'.

Within days a lady came and took the room:
a dressmaker, whose name was Mrs Vaughan.
She and her husband lost everything they had
in the diamond diggings. Just after that,
I was taken ill, my first baby was born,
but of course never lived. As Mrs Vaughan
had typhoid fever, Jack wired for his mother:
she came for a week and was quite kind to me.
Then Frank came to spend his three weeks' leave with us:
he took us to an auction mart, where we bought
sitting room chairs, sofa, and dining-table;

we went with him to cinemas and theatres
and, on the last Saturday, to the racecourse
at Germiston. I had never been before
and never since: it was all so exciting,
quite apart from the most delicious cold lunch
(I'm a pig, I always remember the food).

Frank went back, and soon after Jack's mother wrote:
her husband had left her and she was stranded,
so could she come and live with us? Jack and Bert
said they weren't going to have her in Benoni:
she'd disgrace them. So I asked them what they meant,
and they said: she gets drunk. She'd been kind to me,
so I persuaded them. Bert paid for her keep:
he'd now opened a fruit and grocery shop
with his profits from the Kaffir eating-house.
When the old lady had been with us a year,
she suddenly burst out with her drunkenness:
she'd got some money making milk-jug covers,
and one day two men brought her home in a cab.
She went back to Ivy in Johannesburg.
Bert sent her £1 a week: how she spent it,
on her living or on drink, I couldn't guess.

I'd now been in South Africa for two years,
and we were beginning to get on our feet.
We saved, I did lots of knitting and sewing,
until we had enough for a holiday:
we went to East London for Christmas, staying
with Jack's sister Millie. He had grown up there,
a lovely seaside place with a wonderful beach,
so he knew all about it. But, coming back,
there were lots of Cape policemen in the train:
it looked as though there'd be trouble on the Rand.
Benoni seemed the hottest spot. The miners
were out on strike, the surface men still working,
so Jack went back on Monday. Then they came out,
because the miners were threatening them. Of course,
a few turned up: the miners got hold of them
and thrashed them, while some men at Brakspan mines

were beaten and then thrown down a disused shaft.
Those miners were a proper unruly crowd,
mostly low Dutch, and not satisfied with that:
they broke into houses, tore down the curtains,
dragged out the furniture, set fire to the lot;
so many were left homeless in Benoni.

One morning, about the beginning of March,
we woke to bugles sounding the fall-in call:
it wasn't the Boy Scouts, it was the strikers
preparing for an imminent attack from
the Transvaal Scottish marching for Benoni.
A battle began, martial law was proclaimed,
nobody was allowed out after seven.
There were bullets whizzing up every street
and you daren't put your nose outside the door;
we had no food because the shops were all shut.
I was expecting Dulcie any minute.

Lily, better at recording death than birth,
has nothing to say about 23 March,
apart from a photo of a tree-lined street
and some low municipal buildings, captioned,
'Benoni, where Dulcie was born': my mother.

3

We had quite a houseful while we were shut up:
there were Mrs Vaughan, Bert, Mr Ashington –
they came for refuge while their shop was picketed –
as well as Jack and myself. But luckily
we had a sack of flour, so I could make bread:
no meat for days, just bread, tea and coffee.
We played cards and dominoes and tiddlywinks,
all the games we could think of. General Smuts
sent aeroplanes to drop bombs on us, and then
machine guns from aeroplanes, pop, pop, popping,
meaning to injure the miners but hurting
innocent people instead. Meanwhile, of course,

everyone was getting hungry: so, at night,
they looted the shops. Bert's was one of the first:
we could see men creeping along by the walls,
sacks full of stuff on their backs. And all the shops
in Market Avenue were treated the same,
boots, shoes and clothing as well as food taken,
and what they couldn't take broken or destroyed:
a town ruined, shops spoilt and houses riddled
with bullets, and ambulances tearing past.

It was a Monday morning when the strikers
were whacked: the place was filled with mounted police
and Transvaal Scottish when all of a sudden
a whole army of Free State Burghers appeared,
fierce funny-looking men, and they meant business.
They rounded up the men from every house:
they were driven in flocks like a lot of sheep
by these horrible old Dutchmen on horseback.
It was a boiling hot day, and some were sent
to the police station, while others were packed
into the athletic grounds in the hot sun,
a machine gun trained on them, nothing to eat
or drink. About 6.30 in the evening,
many were sent home, but the rest were detained.

The Beales were the happiest married couple:
they had a darling little boy named Jimmy,
their own house and car, everything they needed.
Mr Beale was detained for nothing at all:
his wife was ill, he was anxious to get back,
so at midnight he took off his boots, climbed out
the window, dodged the guards and was running home,
when he was challenged by some Transvaal Scottish.
He wouldn't stop, so they stabbed him through the heart
with a bayonet and, about the same time,
Mrs Beale had a baby daughter, Molly.
No one knew what had happened to Mr Beale
or where they buried him. When his wife told me,
I was in bed: Dulcie was then three days old,
a lovely fat baby with her dark blue eyes,

black hair, and a line right across her forehead,
just like May had when she cut her head open.

With the strike over, everyone was hard up.
Bert had lost everything and went to Jo'burg
to look for work. We moved to a smaller house,
four rooms and a scullery built in line,
with a wide mosquito-netted verandah,
a delightful place to sit and have our meals:
the floor was red stone with lots of plants in tubs,
a big table and two or three comfy chairs.
There was a gorgeous garden: along one side,
a run for our fowls and, along the other,
peach and plum trees, nectarines, quinces and vines;
in the middle, a lovely flower garden.
Dulcie slept in her pram beneath two peach trees:
she was six weeks when we moved from Bedford Street.
Our neighbours gave her a sweet little puppy,
a cross of Irish setter and Airedale named Pat:
he was a nuisance, but he loved the baby.

Things were still bad. Bert found no work in Jo'burg,
so came back to us: he did the gardening
and took baby out. Saturday afternoons,
we'd go to football: baby would be so good,
lying in the pram bought with my last £5.
And about this time Jack bought a motorbike,
a BSA, on the hire purchase system.
Finally, Bert got a job as manager
of a big store at Geduld Township in Springs,
so when he left us we had Millie and Frank
for their holiday, also Gladys and Gwen.
She is such a marm: she wanted waiting on –
of course, we couldn't afford a Kaffir boy –
and wouldn't lift a finger to do a thing.

A terrible storm began one afternoon,
starting at four o'clock and lasting six hours:
thunder, lightning, and hailstones big as golf balls.
It tore the leaves off the trees, killed the flowers,

and blocked up all the gutterings of the house.
Water streamed down the walls of every room,
wallpaper was torn off and furniture drenched;
I covered all the beds with mackintoshes
to keep them dry for the night. Well, that put an end
to our stay in the house: Jack was determined
we'd find a place that didn't let in water.
Bert persuaded us to move to Springs, near him,
where there were plenty of nice houses to let.

I decided before leaving Benoni
to give Pat back to his previous owners:
with a baby and a four-hour train journey,
I had quite enough to do. Gladys and Gwen
were coming with us too. We all got settled
on the train: it was just leaving the station,
when someone said, 'There's a dog under your seat.'
I looked; to my astonishment, there was Pat,
curled up. I hadn't got a ticket for him;
anyway, dogs had to travel in boxes;
but when the ticket collector came along,
Pat never budged an inch and so wasn't seen.
We had to change at Boksburg. Pat followed me
onto the train but wouldn't lie down again:
he paraded up and down the corridor.
I was told to put him off at the next stop,
but the ticket collector never returned,
and so poor old Pat got to Springs after all.

We were quite all right for a couple of months,
then Jack did a stupid thing. He'd served his time
as an apprentice, but his two years at war
meant he wasn't qualified to take a job
as a journeyman at six guineas a week;
they offered him an improver's job at five,
but he turned it down and said he'd look elsewhere.
That finished him: no mine would take him on now,
and that beastly motorbike from Benoni
wasn't paid for. All we'd saved was £15.
Gwen caught chickenpox and then Dulcie caught it:

she wasn't yet two and was very seedy.
To make matters worse, Gladys and Gwen moved out,
so we had to pay the rent of the whole house.

I was ill and we were down poverty street;
my third baby was born, and the poor mite lived
only eleven hours. We had no money
to pay for a doctor or the burial
of the little child: that bill is still owing
to this day. Jack had spent our last £15,
putting it down on a horse and cart: he said
he would sell vegetables for a living.
As time went on, he began to do quite well –
I really thought we would be able to pay
some of our debts – but in the middle of May
the mornings and evenings became very cold:
getting up early and going to market
didn't please the man. So all of a sudden,
he made up his mind to sell our little home
and make a trek to somewhere warmer: Durban.

Everything was sold at auction: those few pounds
we had to keep to feed us on the journey.
We couldn't pay any of our debts, so Jack
thought he might as well do somebody else down:
a few days before we set off, he ordered
a canopy for the cart, which made it look
like a covered wagon; he'd no intention
of paying for it. Bert threw up his good job
to join us. Otherwise, he said, we'd be killed:
one man couldn't manage a horse and wagon
on those treacherous hilly roads to Durban.
So we stole out like thieves early one morning,
without anyone knowing where we had gone.

*A diary of our big trek, from Springs to Durban, a distance of 483 miles,
taking us exactly 30 days. By one splendid horse named Polly and a
covered trolley.*
Started 5th June 1924
Finished 5th July 1924
*Starting the journey: Bert, Jack, baby and myself, our good old dog Pat
and Miss Kitty.*

Thursday 5th June: We leave Springs at 5.30,
and travel at a good trot, reaching Nigel
at 10.30: we outspan and make a fire
from dry cow dung, an excellent burning fuel,
and have a nice breakfast. We are ravenous,
eating two bacon rashers and two eggs each,
and almost a whole loaf of bread. Thus warmed up,
we all set to work: Bert feeds and grooms Polly,
while Jack and I wash up and put the cart straight.
We travel on to a place called Heidelberg,
arriving at 4.30, where we outspan
by the river. A kind man gives us some wood,
so we make a blazing fire and cook dinner
of grilled chops, wash the dishes and go to bed.
It's rather early and we find we can't sleep
for the strangeness and cold, though Dulcie sleeps well.

Friday 6th June: Bert is first up, makes a fire,
gets the kettle boiling by seven o'clock:
we have tea and toast, then make a good breakfast.
We walk through the town, a pretty little place,
a range of hills beyond and a white stone church,
a high bell tower and clock chiming the hour.
At eleven, we set off for Standerton:
a mile or two out, we strike a nasty hill
and we all have to help push with all our might.
After lunch, the road takes us through many farms
with big gates across the road. In the evening,
we find a lovely spot to camp for the night:
a stream for water, two hills to shelter us.

Saturday 7th June: Bert is up first again.
By about 9.30 we are on the road:
Jack and Bert try to get a few birds to eat,
while Dulcie and I go to sleep – surprising
how sleepy the jog of a cart makes one feel.
At midday, we rest and feed the good old horse,
then trot on, passing the village of Balfour,
and outspan for the night. Bert unpacks the cart,
Jack unharnesses Polly, gives her water,
while Dulcie and I look for some dry cow dung
to start a fire. Well, there isn't very much
just here. So we collect twigs, and then I think
of trying to get some coal from the railway.
As a train draws near, I hold up a small piece
I've found on the line: the driver and stoker
know just what I want and throw some large lumps out.
After a good meal, I put Dulcie to bed,
and then the three of us and our dog and cat
all sit round the lovely coal fire, and even
the good old horse comes trotting to take a look.

Sunday 8th June: We all wake up at sunrise
with the cooing of the doves. Jack is up first
and makes the fire, and we start off on our way
at half past nine. We cover a good distance,
as the road is flat passing through Greylingstad,
but there is no fresh water to be found here:
we have to use the emergency supply
which we always carry in a big stone jar.
When we reach a spring, we outspan for the night,
although it's still only early afternoon.
We have a good wash, and the men their first shave
since we left Springs: they need it very badly.
While we are eating our dinner this evening,
Polly strays and, after a lot of searching,
we find her trotting back the way we have come.

Monday 9th June: Glorious morning sunshine:
we travel hard until two o'clock. Water
is very scarce again, but at last we find

a beautiful river. We make up our minds
to go no further, for Polly needs a rest,
and I've got quite a lot of washing to do.

Tuesday 10th June: Horrors! Polly strays again.
Poor old horse, she may have been trotting all night.
After two hours' search, Bert finds her on a farm
three miles away. Half the morning being gone,
we decide to stop here until after lunch;
so I dry and air my washing on the grass,
mend a hole or two and sew some buttons on.
By dusk, we have reached the town of Standerton:
we find a delightful place to camp, sheltered
by tall blue gum trees, with the big River Vaal
running past us. Just as we're getting settled,
an elderly man and woman come rushing
across the field towards us: 'Get off our land!'
they both shout, but as soon as we speak they know
we aren't poor Dutch and they couldn't be more kind.
They ask us into their house and, when we leave,
give us new laid eggs and a huge jug of milk.

Wednesday 11th June: The old lady sends fresh milk
and hopes we've had a good night. After breakfast,
ready to leave, we find Miss Kitty has gone:
as a rule, she'd have been curled up on the cart
as soon as our blankets and cushions were on.
We had heard a tomcat strolling round the wood
in the night, so we go in there and call her:
Mr Tom comes running, but not Miss Kitty.
We decide to have a last look at the house,
and there she is, sitting on the verandah.
So we set off, passing many Kaffir kraals:
they are allowed to work on a farmer's land
for a quarter share of profits and they build
these pretty little round huts made of rushes,
with a hole for them to crawl through as a door,
like huge beehives. At last we reach Amersfoort,
where it's so bitterly cold and so windy
that baby and I have to stay in the wagon

while the men cook. We have a drop of brandy
to warm us up, but I swear that Jack and Bert
have more than that, for they're joking and laughing
all the time they cook. The dinner is A1.

Thursday 12th June: Kitty is missing again,
so we go on without her. I truly hope
she will find a nice home: she's such a sweet cat.
It is pretty here – there are lots of green trees,
plantations of blue gum trees border the road –
unlike most of the Transvaal, which is bare veldt.
Water is scarce: when we reach a little stream,
we outspan, as it's best to keep near water,
and then roast the wild doves that the men have shot.

Friday 13th June: Misty but not so cold.
An old Boer farmer comes up to chat with us:
we are firing at a target (my first shot
with a rifle, not bad for a beginner).
Then we are off: jogging along till midday,
a little rest, then on once more till sunset.
We outspan by a little stream near Volksrust,
but we don't manage a very good night's rest.
About one o'clock we look out: Polly has strayed.
Bert wakes up to find his mouth is frozen –
he's the coldest, sleeping under the wagon –
so Jack goes off to look for the horse. Meanwhile,
Bert lights our Primus stove and makes some cocoa
to warm us all up, for we're chilled to the bone.

Saturday 14th June: We are on the road
at quarter to ten, cars and traps passing us
on their way to morning market in Volksrust.
Jack takes the horse to be shod, we have our lunch,
then we start off once more: slow this afternoon,
as we have to climb steep hills. We see a train
on a narrow ledge cut into the hillside,
beneath the roadway. At last we travel down,
and camp in the valley where the three hills met,
beside a stream where ferns grow among the rocks.

Sunday 15th June: Fresh after a good night,
we are curious to learn what we shall find
on the other side of the enormous hill
which lies ahead of us. When we reach the top,
we pass through avenues of black wattle trees,
with lovely scent from mimosa-like flowers.
These pretty English-looking lanes take us past
Mujuba Hill, site of the famous battle
in the Boer War: up hill and down dale all day
through the most magnificent country I've seen,
until we reach a river sheltered by trees.

Monday 16th June: We decide to remain
in this ideal spot for the day. After breakfast,
Jack and Bert take the cartwheels off to soak them
in the river. Then we all have a good bathe
and wash our heads. Jack makes brake blocks for the cart,
for we'll soon be reaching some very steep hills,
while Bert, Dulcie and I wash our dirty clothes,
Kaffir-fashion, on the stones in the river.
We have a good dinner: we always eat well.

Tuesday 17th June: On the road once more,
lots of cars passing, fetching farmers to vote
in the nearest town, as it's election day.
Passing through mealie lands, we reach Newcastle
and find our river to outspan for the night.

Wednesday 18th June: Newcastle is busy
after the election as we walk through it.
When we return to the wagon, Pat has gone:
we at last find him wandering round the town
and so start again on our way until dusk.

Thursday 19th June: A bitterly cold night
and an uneventful day. At Danhauser,
where we outspan, there is no grass for Polly:
a poor dry place, but we make the best of it.
Before we go to bed, a boy comes along
and offers to have the horse in his paddock.

Friday 20th June: Up early this morning,
buying food in the village: the cheapest place
we have struck, and everyone seems so friendly.
Through the morning, we travel on even ground –
so even that I take the reins for a time –
before we hit some terrible rocky roads.
In fact, they aren't roads at all, just baboon paths,
a mass of rocks and stones winding round the hills.

Saturday 21st June: Once we are off,
we have more terrible monkey paths to climb.
We outspan for the night inside some farm gates:
it's so warm this evening that I can sit out
beside the camp fire and write two letters home.

Sunday 22nd June: A dusty road
this morning: we pass a coal mine, Kaffir kraals,
then a lot of Boer War graves near Ladysmith.
The town itself we find is rather pretty,
road and railway in the valley, and houses
all built on the hillsides. We stay for the night
on a common full of mimosa bushes.

Monday 23rd June: Polly must be shod,
so Jack takes her into town. We start trekking
again after lunch, but all of a sudden
a terrific wind gets up: we have to stop
and camp there in some very sandy quarters.

Tuesday 24th June: A terrible night,
the wagon almost blown over in the wind
and sand flying about in all directions:
at daybreak, we get away from that desert
but not out of that wind. We reach Colenso.

Wednesday 25th June: Our luck is out:
an awful night with a wicked thunderstorm
and only a few spots of rain. However,
about seven in the morning it rains hard:
we stay put until it clears at eleven.

The dear old sun shines again. After shopping,
we go off the main road to take a short cut,
very close to the border of Zululand.
We pass a tribe of men going to battle,
youngest to oldest, all armed, with their war paint,
assegais and shields: I suppose they've quarrelled
and are going to fight it out. From our camp,
we hear in the distance a native wedding:
they sing all the time for three days and three nights.
It is such a ghastly noise: their throats must ache.

Thursday 26th June: A lovely morning:
the wind drops, the sun is beautifully warm.
And birds: canaries galore! Well, off we go,
through pretty country, but such a rocky road,
and all uphill. Target practice after lunch:
I beat both the men. We wonder when we'll strike
the main road, and we tell ourselves we'll never
take short cuts again, for they take twice as long.
At sunset, we meet the road: after a mile,
we find a good spot to outspan for the night.
Everyone we speak to, even Kaffir boys,
marvels at our willing and wonderful horse,
who's pulled us and our load all the way from Springs.

Friday 27th June: The road is nice and smooth,
so Polly starts at a good pace. We soon reach
Estcourt, where our best bacon and sausages
come from, a lovely little place with clean streets.
Jack goes to the shop to buy mealies and bran
for Polly's feed. We have a terrible hill
to climb from this town: it seems never-ending.
We find some water, stop a couple of hours,
then up more hills on a pass cut round the side.
The sun shines down on gorgeous flowers and ferns,
hillsides above us, water rushing below.
We outspan by a blue gum tree plantation.

Saturday 28th June: At every bend,
we find we have to climb higher still, until

at last we reach the top and a steep road down.
We're quite near the end of this when Polly trips
and begins to limp. We stop and bathe the knee,
before moving on to find a resting-place:
this is Mooi River, and the little town
named after it is noted for its butter.

Sunday 29th June: We have our breakfast,
without hurrying, so that Polly can rest.
While we are sitting there, a chicken turns up:
it's the only one about and it's so tame
that Jack decides we'll have to take it with us.
We haven't anything to eat for dinner,
and as it's a Sunday the shops will be shut.
What a wicked thing to do! Yet on the road,
it seems as though it were a gift from the gods,
knowing that we should go hungry otherwise.
So we set off again with more hills to climb:
cows and sheep grazing on their sides, and below,
a stream between plantations of black wattle.
We outspan for the night in a sheltered spot,
then make a fire and roast the little chicken
in our good three-legged Kaffir cooking-pot:
a delicious meal, though stolen property.

Monday 30th June: It seems so funny:
although the drop is almost 6,000 feet
from Johannesburg to the sea at Durban,
we are always going uphill. However,
at last the road is getting fairly level
as we pass through very English-looking lanes
to reach the pretty health resort of Howick,
which is famous for its lovely waterfalls.
Here I see oranges, lemons and nartjies
(tangerines at home) growing for the first time.
We find a nice place to camp by the river,
but the grass is rather long and I'm afraid
of meeting a snake, even though the men say
they will never show themselves in the winter.

Tuesday 1st July: There are many more trees
growing in Natal: everything is so green.
Hydrangeas are growing wild on the hillsides,
and aloes with fibrous trunks, watery leaves,
red flowers at the top. We have to go down
a tremendous hill to Pietermaritzburg:
we are coming level with the railway line,
a train with three engines steaming towards us.
There are big houses in beautiful gardens,
looking tropical, with bamboos and huge palms,
and plenty of well-dressed people. What a state
of excitement Dulcie is in: such a change
from the veldt and hills! She's never seen a tram
until now. On the other side of the town,
we find a good place to outspan for the night.

Wednesday 2nd July: Lovely and fresh,
with another hill to climb: flat road after that.
It's so hot, we have to rest by a river
for two or three hours before carrying on
to flatter land with fields and fields of mealies,
and a few of barley or wheat, nice and green
between the yellow mealies. We are quite late
on the road, as we haven't found water:
we trot on, through clouds of warm and then cold air,
but still no water. Entering Camperdown,
Bert asks a Zulu boy to fetch us water:
he brings us two bucketsful, and new laid eggs
at a shilling a dozen. After dinner,
it's warm enough for us to sit without coats
for the first time since we began our journey.

Thursday 3rd July: One more tremendous hill;
on the other side, blue gum tree plantations
being hewn down, as far as the eye can see.
We come to 'The Valley of a Thousand Hills',
and then another climb: this road is a ledge
turning round and round the hill, with no water.
At dusk, we come across some road repairmen,
four whites, several natives: the whites are drunk.

They won't give us water, but they offer drink
to Bert and Jack, who refuse: they are horrid,
and I'm really quite scared. So we carry on,
reaching a place called Hillcrest: there is water
from the power station and we have our meal,
then after a long day settle for the night.

Friday 4th July: We find a lovely spot,
a precious stream and wonderful shady trees,
where we have a bathe and do all the washing;
for we're nearing Durban, the end of our trek.
We remain here until about four o'clock,
then travel on: there are bananas,
pineapples and paw paw; fields of sugar cane
stretching for miles. Close to an Indian school,
we stop for the night, with the lights of Durban
and the lighthouse flickering in the distance.

Saturday 5th July: Just before we leave,
the Indian schoolmaster brings us a bowl
of freshly picked oranges. Hundreds of cars
are passing us on their way to Durban races
for the July Handicap, so on we trot,
all the way to the racecourse and outspan there,
like gypsies at the Derby, and watch the race.
In the evening, Bert takes me to see Durban,
while Jack looks after Dulcie, who is asleep.
We take a tram to the beach – it is high tide,
huge breakers coming over the esplanade –
then back in a rickshaw, a rubber-tyred cart
with a barefooted Kaffir boy pulling us.
He is dressed to kill: a pair of bullock's horns
stuck on his head, decorated with feathers
and flowers, and a goatskin round his shoulders.
Eventually we arrive back at our home,
the wagon, and have our usual good night's sleep.

5

Next day, we travelled up the coast of Natal,
close to the mouth of the Umgeni River,
where we found a place to camp on a sand-dune,
bushy trees forming a half-circle round us,
a salt water pool – the Blue Lagoon – in front,
and the great Indian Ocean beyond it.
We spent all July out in the open there,
leading a healthy bushman's life, with free rent,
free wood, free water, catching fish, shooting birds:
it really is the way we were meant to live.
But we knew that soon we'd have to find a home.

Eventually, we found two unfurnished rooms
in a house shared with some Malayan people.
The floors were stone, and we had no furniture:
we had to put the mattresses on the floor,
and make the best of it. We tethered Polly
on a piece of nearby ground; within a week,
she got free and broke her leg. We had her shot.
I felt dreadful: she had been a faithful friend
and worked hard. Bert went back to Johannesburg
to find a job: he had been a good friend too.
Jack sold the wagon for only a few pounds
to help us along until he could find work.
Dulcie became ill with a high temperature.
I got rheumatism in my feet and legs –
it was sleeping on the stone floor, I suppose –
and couldn't put on my shoes. We all had colds.
Dulcie recovered, though she did look seedy,
but I couldn't walk and Jack didn't bother:
he made no effort at all to find a job.

I'd struggle to the verandah for fresh air
and watch people waiting for trams to Durban.
One morning a man called down to me and said:
'I've seen you there for weeks and can't understand
why you're living in a coloured person's house.
It isn't done here. Are you in need of help?'

I said I'd give anything to get away,
but we had nothing. He promised to call in:
he worked for the Governor General Fund.

When I told Jack what I'd done, he wasn't pleased.
But I said we couldn't go on living there,
in that damp place, without a bed to lie on,
nor a table or chair, while he did nothing
to get us out of the mess. When the man came,
he was horrified. He told Jack he'd help us
get back to Johannesburg and, next morning,
he'd take Dulcie and me to the Fund's office.
So Jack wrote then and there to Bert, asking him
to find us a room, and the following morning
the man hired a rickshaw for Dulcie and me
(in Jack's bedroom slippers) to go to the Fund.
There they said that they would send for us again
as soon as we heard Bert had found us a room.
A week later, he wrote to say he had done so:
in a suburb of Jo'burg called Wolhuter,
with a German woman, Mrs Robertson.
He'd also bought us beds, as he couldn't bear
the thought of us sleeping on the floor again.
I went to the Governor General Fund
and told them: they had railway and food tickets
for Jack and me, but there weren't baby tickets,
so the man gave me £1 from his pocket
to buy her food. What kindness from a stranger!

Our new room was spotlessly clean, with bare boards,
two iron beds and curtains at the window.
Mrs Robertson lent us table and chairs
until we could buy our own. Such poverty!
We had only a couple of pounds for food;
Bert had paid our first month's rent. Every midday,
this sweet German woman brought Dulcie a meal.
She had two little boys: when they had their lunch,
Dulcie had hers too. Jack's only comment was:
'Anyone would think I can't afford her food.'
I replied: 'You can't, and she can't take pot luck

like us.' At last my feet were getting better:
I could put my own shoes on again. But Jack
still hadn't found work, although he was looking.
By now, even my wedding ring had been pawned:
I used to sit and think how silly I'd been
to leave England for this place, and then I'd think
I couldn't have been so terribly wicked
that God would want me and my baby to starve.
We had been there a month and the rent was due.
A few days later, a letter came from home:
Dad, sensing all wasn't well, enclosed five pounds,
a tidy sum for him, a godsend for us.

Then Jack got a job with the Parks Department:
not what he wanted, though better than nothing.
It was good to get back to normal living,
a weekly wage coming in, and every week
we managed to buy some piece of furniture:
we started going to auction rooms again.
Jack met a few friends while we were living there:
a blacksmith, Fred Holton, and Eileen Goldsmith,
an old girlfriend of his. But after six months,
he decided we should move into Jo'burg,
nearer his work. He found an unfurnished room
in Bree Street, at the bottom of the garden
of a big house: he preferred his own front door.
He soon got fed up with gardening and said
he was sure that he could make a tea-room pay:
so he borrowed the money from Fred Holton
to rent a shop at the top end of Bree Street.
He fixed it up with a few tables and chairs,
a counter for fruit and sweets and cigarettes,
and then we duly opened. I worked and worked
to keep the place clean, even cleaning windows,
which was something a white woman never did.
There weren't many customers. I did breakfasts
for the rooms over the shop, just tea and toast,
and each morning I used to take the trays up;
we sold quite a lot of sweets and cigarettes,
but no teas or coffees, where the money was.

After four months, we couldn't pay the warehouse:
in desperation, I wrote to Bert for help.
He came on the night train to Johannesburg,
took one look at the books and said: 'You must go:
just pack a few things and do a moonlight flit.'
He went for Jack for being such a wastrel:
why couldn't he work and keep his wife and child
in a proper manner? He told us to leave
Saturday night by the Pretoria train,
change for Naboomspruit, wait till Monday,
then take the train to where he worked at Crecy:
it was just a little halt among large farms,
on the border of Southern Rhodesia.
Bert ran the huge corrugated iron store,
with everything from a needle to a plough,
also post office and telephone exchange:
alongside, there was a bedroom, living-room,
and improvised kitchen; no water or light.
There were oil lamps; water was fetched from a well
two hundred yards away, in paraffin tins,
by Martin the native boy, on a barrow.
So this was the place that we were going to.

6

At last we were aboard the train to Crecy,
a little Puffing Billy kind of engine
and three trucks – one for whites and two for coloureds –
with forms on either side and canvas flapping:
it ran twice a week, the days for meat and mail.
So we jolted along through miles of rough veldt,
all very dry and dusty, until we reached
the Crecy siding. A hundred yards away
stood the huge iron store. We got settled in.
Bert told Jack what to do: he would get £5
a month, which wasn't much but was his to save,
because our food and clothing would come from stock
and Bert would pay from his share of the profits.
I learnt to run the post office for train days:

it seemed as though the world and his wife arrived
from all the farms round about, in mule carts, cars,
or with ox wagons. We had to shut the shop
while we sorted the mail; then they'd all swarm in
to get their letters, stamps and postal orders.

The rest of the week we only had a few
straggling natives: they'd walk miles from their kraals,
buy a pair of boots, then walk a little way
and take them off again, tie them together,
sling them over their shoulders and go barefoot.
One day a boy came in to buy a blanket:
Bert spent three hours getting every blanket
off the shelves, then he said he didn't want one.
Bert went for him in his Basuto language,
clicking his tongue, until one of his false teeth
flew out of his mouth and over the counter.
The boy was terrified: he ran from the shop,
screaming and yelling and expecting the tooth
to pursue him. That settled the argument.
We had a good laugh, folding up the blankets.

Some of the people who came in on mail days
used to invite Dulcie and me to their farms.
I also became quite friendly with the girl
on the Naboomspruit telephone exchange,
although I'd never seen her; we would discuss
gramophone records. She'd put on the latest,
and play it through the telephone: 'Tea for Two',
'Valencia', 'I'll Be Loving You Always'.

At the tennis court near the railway siding,
farmers would come and play: we made a foursome
with our nearest neighbour, Captain Sanderson.
He lived alone in a farmhouse with his boy,
Franz, to do for him: it was a pretty place,
made from two rondavels for the two main rooms.
I also kept chickens for an interest,
starting with a dozen hens and a rooster.
I never cooped them up: they wandered the veldt,

eating grubs and insects, but came home to roost
at night, when I gave them a good feed of corn.
There was one white hen the men had named Lily:
they said she took after me, spruce and fussy;
if she could get into my bedroom, she would,
and then lay her egg on my bed. However,
after a time I shut the door and window:
then she laid her eggs under a mimosa,
where we couldn't reach and, having laid thirteen,
sat on them and brought out thirteen lovely chicks.
There was one little chick that would lag behind,
so poor old Pat (we still had him) used to go
and help it with a gentle push from his paw.
One day, a hawk swooped and caught this little one,
but Lily flew up and fought till he dropped it:
I put Vaseline on it and cared for it,
and it was fit again in a day or two.
One by one my hens were all going broody:
I called one, a busybody, Mrs Dixon,
while Milly was easy and comfortable,
and in the end I had hundreds of chickens.

We had a plague of locusts like a black cloud:
they settled on Captain Sanderson's mealie,
just coming up, and ate all the young green shoots.
They were horrible-looking things, and their wings
made an unbelievable noise when they flew.
Then there were ants. White ones would eat through a sack
in a night and right through our carpet as well;
black ones, bigger than in England, really bite
if they get on you, and there's a big red ant.
After it had rained, they all grew wings and flew
until their wings dropped off, and then you'd find them
crawling around. And such huge spiders that sting!
I met some very strange insects at Crecy.

The siding further up from us was Truro:
Harry and Lily Lawe managed a farm there.
He was something to do with the Scout movement,
and one weekend he went to Johannesburg

for a dinner honouring Baden Powell,
who was visiting South Africa just then.
He didn't like to leave his wife in the farmhouse,
surrounded by native kraals, so he asked me
to spend the weekend with her. Dulcie and I
caught the little train to Truro one Friday:
it was quite a treat to live in a real house,
well furnished with lovely kitchen and bathroom.
They had five Alsatians, Molly and Roland,
and three puppies: Dulcie loved them and they her.
We slept with revolvers under our pillows,
and were very glad we had them and the dogs,
for we were the only white people for miles.
Friday was quiet; Saturday and Sunday,
the natives got drunk on beer – the noise they made
was quite eerie at times, and we were both pleased
to see Harry step off the train on Monday.
We caught its return journey, back to Crecy.

There was a whirlwind: we could see it coming
miles away, picking up the dry sandy earth.
We went into the shop and shut all the doors,
but the wind took my improvised kitchen –
pots, pans, kettles, basins, teacloths, everything –
and blew it over the veldt. When it died down,
we had to go searching for our belongings;
the air was stifling, with a smell of red sand
for days, until eventually the rains came.

Martin brought a baby jackal for Dulcie:
he was such a nice boy and so fond of her,
and he thought that she would like him as a pet.
He was a little grey fluffy animal,
with a pointed nose, and he loved being nursed,
but as he grew older he became spiteful;
we couldn't put up with bites from his sharp teeth,
so we took him for a walk to Twee Kopjes,
where there were jackals (we could hear them at night),
and let him go back to his natural friends.

1926. And there the journal ends:
blank white pages in a black-covered notebook
conceal Jack's rages and Lily's departure;
her funding a passage home (Bert helped, of course)
by working at the Singer sewing machine
in the attic above me now; her return
to London and her going into service
at Overstrand Mansions – a single mother,
with a four-year-old daughter – in Battersea.

The Gardener

1950

She starts almost from scratch. The garden sleeps,
Wrapped in a fallow blanket of neglect.
Rhubarb and horseradish silently erupt;
A long pale wound of birch-bark peels and weeps.

Experience will mend her early errors –
The rockery wall, the crazy-paving terrace
And fads for floribunda roses, dahlias –
Until this heavy acre holds no terrors.

The Flower Show awards her every trophy
(She likes the praise but hates the polishing).
There's fruit enough for eating and preserving;
Her kitchen garden yields unrationed plenty.

The child, who thinks his tricycle a bus,
Selects a tree-stump for its terminus.

1958

A reclamation job, this garden: planned
Through long Edwardian summers, gone to seed;
The children and the grandchildren of weed
Have colonised it as their promised land.

Slowly, outlines reappear: the rockery
Tumbles down to an overshadowed pond;
Apple and plum trees screen steep fields beyond;
Her cricket team of poplars lines the boundary.

Now terraced lawns sport freshly-printed stripes;
Pots and parterres wear their autumn shades;
And later, when the worst of winter fades,
The dell fills up with snowdrops, aconites.

Cycling along the drive, her son's at ease,
Blessed with confetti from the cherry trees.

1964

This garden's ready-made: another hill
Climbs to a Kentish oasthouse, while below
Walled steps and grassy terraces fall to
An ancient cottage named after its well.

With middle age comes order, and a diary.
She notes the sowing, planting, potting-on.
Dust carrots with soot. Give beans a lime solution.
Camellia buds are stripped or dropped: too dry.

Prune and shape Miss Jessup's Upright: April.
Divide and plant hepatica (two survived).
All the Patchwork Rarities annuals germinated.
Plant Wedding Day rambler by the Bramley apple.

The lanky boy, hunched over handlebars,
Pedals down the road, dreaming of cars.

1989

She starts again from scratch: a grassy mess.
By late November: *Garden rotovated,*
Paths and paving laid and pond constructed.
Here she creates her structured wilderness:

Shrubs and herbs; a fig tree by the wall;
Silver Jerusalem sage against red berberis;
Grey dappled light of sorbus; purple clematis.
Two drunken Irish yews stand sentinel.

The shadows lengthen. First her husband dies,
Then memory falters, joints become arthritic:
To spade and fork she adds a walking-stick.
Yet still she tends and prunes; the garden thrives.

She wills her own green burial: she knows
That what we plant outlives us, and outgrows.

Shutting Down

'We've moved her,' they say, 'to a single room.
We thought she would be more comfortable.'
I read their faces to decode what this means:
Her condition would distress the other patients.

Driving in, this placid summer evening,
I prayed: let it be one thing or the other,
A proper recovery or a rapid end,
Anything but unwilling, lingering half-life.

She no longer tries to speak as I hold her hand,
Until shaken by a cough trapped in her throat.
I run for help, but the words 'death rattle' check me.
'She just decided,' says the sister, 'to shut down.'

A Huntingdonshire Elegy

In memory of Rod Shand

How typical of you to disappear like that:
Nothing packed, wallet and house-keys left,
Just going for a stroll. So here's a caveat:

A double existence out of Greene or le Carré
Is something you might plausibly possess.
Your life's disguises seem to twinkle: 'Solve me!'

You were a riddle from the day I heard of you,
Bored, out of my depth, at my first staff meeting,
Where dull men grumbled on about no one I knew.

'What does one say to a boy who spends his summer
Touring the brothels of Latin America?'
Silence, then: 'Ask for the addresses, Headmaster.'

This I must meet, I thought. And luck had me teaching
'General English' to the upper science sixth,
As if someone supposed they needed civilising.

Some did; but you, the biologist from Bogotá,
Introduced me to your Spanish talisman,
The 'Pequeño Poema Infinito' of Lorca.

At Christmas and Easter, though it seemed illegal,
You didn't go home but took a flat in Cambridge.
We roamed the colleges, drank in the Eagle,

And talked and talked of books. One afternoon you
Inscribed to me your first edition Márquez:
'Winner of the Shand Peace Prize, 1972.

'Love, Roddy.' Now I picture you in Staughton,
Purple tee-shirted, sprawled in my Lurashell chair,
Urgently telling me what next to fix my mind on,

64

Or in Colombian poncho at the thatched Crown
('Good evening, duckie,' grinned a friendly old local);
A few days afterwards, the little pub burnt down.

In your interview to read Marine Biology
At Queens', you said you'd sooner go to Bangor.
'Why?' they asked, aghast. 'Because it's got some sea.'

Land of my fathers! I thought of you at the edge
Of your academic ocean, nursing draught Guinness
When you rang from a pub across the Menai Bridge,

Or writing long letters from Neuadd Emrys Evans –
I treasured that name's triple-decker Welshness –
On marine secrets: tomato pips and waste remains.

Next you were off to the Susversity of Unisex
To work on your doctorate: when we met in Lewes
I sensed – was it boredom or something more complex?

Hard to tell, but the thesis remained unfinished.
One chilly Easter week, we went to Aldeburgh,
My own adopted coast. And then you vanished.

It was years before I heard from you again,
Until, on a May evening, there you were in Derby,
Once more feeding coins into a greedy pub phone:

Married, working for British Rail, and worrying
(You said) about your Guinness getting cold.
This seemed both unexpected and unsurprising,

True to a form I was beginning to understand:
So when you and Judy moved to Silicon Valley,
A plush village address in Berkshire commuter-land,

No doubt I should have guessed that wouldn't last.
An unexplained resurfacing at St Andrews, Malta,
Seemed altogether more your style. Years passed.

Then you were running a restaurant in Vancouver
And doing some part-time teaching at the aquarium.
But was this a reinvention or a cover?

It's early summer: perhaps in that other life you're
Sipping a cocktail now in Moscow or Montreal,
As the scent of beanfields wafts over Staughton Moor.

Point-to-Point

In memory of Bill Richardson

Broadoak it was, Dickie Severn and the rest,
Campers and champers on Easter Monday,
Rollers and Land Rovers, ludicrous picnics;
Losing bets on horses, too, of course.
And the booze! Sandy, red-faced, in his element,
Impervious to us, the ironic young,
Stifling our delight at the silliness of it all.

That's forty years ago: more, probably.
And when, a decade later, I caught sight of you,
Owlishly tight in the White Hart one night
Among the gas lamps and the invasive vines,
I knew that I knew you from somewhere else,
A former life, and what's more you knew me.

Less simple than it sounds, this sort of knowing:
Your mind (and why you bludgeoned it) acute
Beyond what's bearable. Examples? Certainly.
Scroll on another ten to a windy spring,
Aldeburgh again, my annual writing visit,
Yet different this time: I'd not meant to be alone.
You saw that at once, although I'd never said.
'Boyfriend stood you up?' you asked. 'Thought so.'
(Which, Adam, was why you had to come next year.)

Scroll on again to when you met my mother:
Your courtesy impeccable, always 'Mrs Powell'.
Now you seemed like a prep-school headmaster
Or stooping clergyman, knowing yet remote:
'Charming lady,' you said, 'but unimaginative.'
And yes, it had baffled me all my life, her lack
Of interest in what went on in others' heads,
Including (I need hardly add) my own.

Inseparable, of course, from those terrible dogs:
That's you with the whippet on *A Halfway House*,
Battling your way along Crag Path into the mist,
Guy's painting so much more evocative than this.
Drunk in David's Place, alarm-clock in your pocket,
Dog on a dressing-gown cord, while the old rascal
Poured after-hours Scotch by his pencil-torchlight:
Never quite my thing, though I saw that for you
It recalled fifties Soho, at Muriel's, or Mabel's.
You'd history there – I remember Stephen Spender
Cutting you dead over some unhealed old wound –
From the days when you'd been a promising poet.

Tunbridge Wells, absurdly, was your family home
Until that Christmas and the terrible accident
At Snape crossroads, in which your brother died:
You came to Suffolk then and never went back.
It's no distance from here to there: a couple of hours
Will do it on a good day, yet I know how it seemed
Another world. Seems so still: that immense
Gradually unravelling distance to the finishing line.